The

Crowning Winner
Inside of Me

The Crowning Winner Inside of Me

10 PRINCIPLES OF LIFE COACHING ADVICE

Kimberly L. Bonnell

Founder and Executive Director of the Miss US Inner
Beauty Pageant

authorHOUSE®

AuthorHouse™
1663 Liberty Drive
Bloomington, IN 47403
www.authorhouse.com
Phone: 1-800-839-8640

Published by AuthorHouse   07/12/2012

ISBN: 978-1-4772-4116-5 (sc)
ISBN: 978-1-4772-4115-8 (e)

DEDICATION

There was a man who walked the face of the Earth 2000 years ago who came to teach us universal laws and principles. The things I have learned written in this book came from discipleship to Him, Jesus Christ.

At His death, Jesus' persecutors mocked Him by placing a crown of thorns upon His head, but He never wavered in His beliefs for our sake. He endured till the end so that I (and you) may know what it is to have abundant and everlasting life. Perhaps that is why I am drawn to pageants—crowns innately remind me of what Jesus did.

Therefore, I dedicate this book to my Heavenly Father, who sent His son Jesus Christ to us, who is King. My Heavenly Father is my relationship of inspiration—and the crowning winner inside of me—for it is through Him I draw my strength.

CONTENTS

Principle #1: Build a core foundation of achieving goals by respecting yourself, others, and the Earth

Getting started . . . When I studied for certification as a life coach it taught the qualities one should posses as a teacher; how to be relatable to others, and a few general principles that could be applied towards achieving goals. What it did not teach was a strategy or a specific "how to" guide that would enable me to teach a "formula" to help others achieve their dreams. It was disappointing because I realized if I wanted to be inspirational I would have to design my own plan and I did not know where to begin. I felt unprepared and underqualified. It wasn't easy because I had to think through what has made me a positive person.

When I began brainstorming and was able to start writing a preliminary outline, I became enlightened as to why the university I attended structured teaching the life coaching series in this manner. It is because achieving dreams is a personal journey. We each stand alone with our own vision; our visions varying, but what may be in sync universally is the connection we have to *ourselves, each other,* and the *Earth*. It is how we care for these relationships that enables us to achieve our dreams.

What I have discovered is the relationship we have with ourselves *first* gives us the innate intuitiveness for all others. It gives us the ability to sustain an open heart to discover ourselves, to understand others, and to respect the Earth. This must be the core foundation of achieving dreams.

Relationships are all powerful because it enables us to tap into something greater than what we are at the moment. That "something" is the vision of what we want to become. We are connecting to a higher self. Therefore, what the university was trying to teach me was to question how well I knew myself to enable me to become more (aware) of who I envision myself to be. This is the basis of achieving any goal. So I realized I *had* been given the tools of a comprehensive plan in teaching others how to ascertain their goals.

Again, when we connect to a vision, we connect to something greater than what we are at the moment and it makes our destiny endless. It is exciting to think our potential is limitless and boundless when we dream. As earlier stated, if we seek a greatness more than what we are at the moment, it connects us to something more powerful in the universe. This "power", or what I call inspiration, can either be from an individual or from a higher presence within our universe. My belief system calls this higher presence God.

What is the meaning of inspiration? It is the need we have for others to help us grow into the person we want to become. The definition of "others" includes God.

To say it in another way, it is the people along the way that provides us with an example, knowledge, and/or opportunity to achieve our dreams.

Our capacity to grow is mind boggling once we grasp our positive energy connects with something greater in the universe when we dream.

We can achieve our dreams by enabling ourselves to grow into our greatness or our potential by nurturing ourselves from the knowledge gained from someone that already possesses it. Again, this could cither be from a higher universal presence (meaning God), or from an individual.

Inspiration from others is a means to connect your life to a higher universal presence.

Anytime you are becoming your higher self by learning from someone at the level of awareness or intelligence you are trying to achieve, it is connecting your dreams to a higher presence because you have connected your life to something greater within someone else that they possess, to realize your higher purpose. To demonstrate, if you wanted to become a doctor, you would attend medical school, thus, you are given the knowledge to become a doctor *through* this individual by their teaching.

Inspiration that is realized from a universal presence, this can be defined as realizing your higher purpose through connecting your dreams *directly to* a universal presence as a result of a relationship to the universe and yourself and not with others.

To recap, inspiration from others is the avenue that helps you grow as a person that directs us *to* a higher presence.

Inspiration from a universal presence is the avenue that helps you grow as a person that is directly *from* a higher power.

To redefine inspiration in a different way, it is the need for God.

It also means it is a dream that no one has ever dreamed before, in which, God is your source for strength.

To use the analogy of inspiration from a universal presence in application, there have been many profound events in history that have heralded many progressive thinkers. Of course this meant they were ahead of their time. Since they were ahead of their time, they needed a source of strength; someone that was more evolved than what they were to connect with (to continue their capacity for growth and to be able to receive direction for their life).

I suspect since their dream was original, there were no individuals they could connect with whom they could draw strength from, again, since they were dreaming a dream no one had ever dreamed before. With whom does a person talk to or communicate with if no predecessors existed with their school of thought? Therefore, the presence of someone they sought after to draw strength from must have been with a divine presence due to their capability to think higher than what could be found within humanity . . . . but could be found with a higher presence.

What happens if you share the same dream with someone? To use the analogy of inspiration from a universal presence on a less grander scale, it also means helping to fulfill *any* dream (not just fulfilling a dream that is original). Any dream, even when shared with others, has significant value and magnitude because no one dream is accomplished in quite the same way. To restate, even though you may share the same dream with someone, such as becoming a doctor, you will not achieve it in quite the same way. Why? Due to a person's particular circumstances, biology, and/or culture. Therefore, the difference that lies within these two types of inspiration is through the type of connection made for inspiration (to achieve their dream).

The type of inspiration that is used as an example in the above paragraph would be accomplished through an individual. Why is it an individual and not directly from a higher presence? Since it is a same or shared dream, it would only be accomplished through others. Let me explain this in a different way.

Where the difference lies between a shared dream or a dream that is original is through the method used for the manifestation of knowledge that is sought. Someone with a shared dream, such as the example provided in a previous paragraph of becoming a doctor, knowledge is gained through the inspiration from others through teaching. If knowledge is sought after from the origin of an original dream, it would be through a higher universal presence.

To make it simpler understood, a shared dream could be two people who both want the same thing, such as becoming a doctor who may or may not accomplish it in quite the same way. If there are differences between these two individuals, it would lie in the way they did not accomplish their dream. To illustrate, if both individuals wanted to become a doctor, they both may attend medical school gaining the same knowledge, but not attend the same university. Why (and how) this would *not* be an original dream is because more than one person wants the same thing.

Someone with an original dream, inspiration would be from a higher universal presence that is gained through enlightenment, which is discovered by *one* individual. An example of this would be a scientist who discovered a cure for a particular disease.

Should credit be given to the higher universal presence for the cure? Did the scientist receive the knowledge for the cure from it and not from intense labor from his own hands? For me, credit should only be given to a universal presence in helping the scientist understand how things *should* work. The scientist is the one who figured out how to solve its physiological abnormality to bring it back to its original (normal) state. This is enlightenment.

In other words, credit should only be given to a higher universal presence for the *use* of finite or exact knowledge, that can be learned on their own with a relationship to the universe or through someone that teaches the individual that will enable a person to solve problems.

The particular problem a person chooses to solve is their enlightenment or "niche".

Whatever they solve is their discovery.

An original dream could be expressed by this formula:

Knowledge + Enlightenment = Discovery

or

Understanding how a body should operate + The desire to use the specific knowledge gained to solve a problem; this could be called a "niche" = Discovery; this could be called an original dream

To express it more clearly, a person's "niche" is what identifies whether it is a shared dream or original dream.

Almost all original dreams begin as a shared dream (originating from finite or exact knowledge that more than one person can obtain). It is a person's intellect, not intelligence, that develops it from a shared dream to an original dream.

Intellect is the ability to understand each other or the depth of compassion we have for humanity.

Intelligence is our capacity, how much or how capable we are of using the ability of intellect, to understand one another. When our intellect is limited, we only achieve shared dreams (please understand though, a person may have a shared dream and their intellect not be limited because not everyone chooses to have an original dream).

Our lack of intellect limits our understanding to the complexities of life that can only be explained (solved) by a higher universal presence, as a higher universal presence is limited in helping us understand life's complexities due to our lack of intellect.

Our lack of intellect can be caused by our environment, culture, and/or religion. Our intellect can be restricted, compressed, and/or stunted in growth because of these variables. As a result, a higher universal presence must help us to understand things through what we know. In other words, a higher universal presence must meet us where we are and woes us to develop our higher self, to bring us into a higher knowledge that will develop ourselves into a relationship of inspiration.

A relationship of inspiration is connecting to (a universal presence through) others or connecting directly to a higher power that will enable you to achieve your dreams.

The more we seek a higher self, the more we can know a universal presence because a universal presence can then reveal itself to us on a deeper level.

What is inspiration not? It is *not* trying to become something from someone else's vision for your life. It is *not* living a dream that someone else has for you other than what YOU can see for yourself. Living out your dream is what *you* want to accomplish through the inspiration of others and/or God. Remember inspiration means to find within another an example, knowledge, or opportunity to achieve your dreams. It can mean one or all three of these things.

To understand inspiration fully, you must also understand that God only gives us the *ability* to dream. But *what* we dream is in relation to who we are through our biology and what is inherent to us from ancestry that is manifested in personal individualism. And please note it is the use of our ability that allows our dreams to become a reality.

What prevents us from using our ability to dream is from (re)occurring negativity or (self) doubt (by others) that destroys the development of ourselves, that ultimately affects our knowledge of a universal God.

It is inspiration then that is the key toward continued motivation to develop ourselves.

Developing ourselves then is the key that gives us the ability to respect ourselves, others, and the Earth, which is the core foundation of principle number one that bleeds into Principle #2.

NOTES

Principle #2: Take care of your mind, body, and soul

We are a trinity of mind, body, and soul. We should take great care with each because one affects the other. But I believe there is an order in which we should assume this awesome responsibility. As I expressed with Principle #1, you should first explore the soul (our relationships). This will connect us to an understanding of our minds (our desires, wants and needs) that manifests itself in the outward expression of the care given to our bodies, others, and the Earth.

Let's discuss the importance of the care that should be given to our mind, bodies, others, and the Earth by examining each one.

The mind is responsible for our thoughts, perceptions, emotions, will, memory, and imagination. Therefore, it is important to renew the mind by providing it with positive input. Whatever you want to believe about yourself and others should be reflective in repetitive statements made to your psyche because whatever your input is, the output will be the same. It takes work to conquer negative self perceptions. It may seem ridiculous to look in the mirror each morning, telling yourself you love who you are, but if you continuously tell yourself positive affirmations, you will begin to believe them. The benefit of loving yourself will result in the ability to love others because you will come to an understanding or appreciation for humanity because you will understand *your* worth.

Secondly, loving yourself will give you the ability to grow as a person or to achieve your dreams because it will give you the confidence to believe in your abilities.

You can nurture confidence by making up cards, taping them in conspicuous places that will remind you of the belief you have in yourself in what it is you are trying to achieve. For example, if one of your goals in life is to complete a marathon as mine is, you should leave yourself notes exclaiming the fact you are a successful runner.

It is also worth mentioning the difference between confidence and ability. When you are attempting to achieve a dream, it is important to understand whether what it is you desire matches your ability. If you are dreaming of becoming a famous singer, but yet your ability only has the potential for local theater, it may be wise to train your voice longer before attempting professionalism of such grandeur. Please do not misinterpret this. I am not propagating discouragement toward any dream a person may have because I believe any dream is possible. But sometimes we forget what achieving a dream is. Achieving a dream is the art of discipline towards a desired result, which takes work, and not the disillusion of "fame". You may be able to muster all of the confidence in the world, but without skill you may fail. You must be prepared.

Confidence means respect for yourself that includes, but not limited to, belief in your abilities.

The formula for success is:

Confidence + Ability = Opportunity for achievement.

Healthy Diet

Eating right is important to not cause any physiological degradation within our bodies. The new food pyramid suggests we eat six ounces of grains, two to five cups of vegetables, two cups of fruits, three cups of milk, and five and one half ounces of meat, fish, and/or beans. Keeping the health of my body in mind, I eat the suggested servings of food on the pyramid. But at times I do overeat by snacking when I am bored, when I am watching television, or when I am working, such as when I am writing (yes, I just polished off some potato chips!). I also have a tendency to indulge in desserts to an unhealthy extent. It takes self-control for me to make the right choices because at times I admit I binge.

When I am most in balance I drink a fruit smoothie for breakfast. I throw two or three cups of fresh fruit and twenty four ounces of milk in a blender, sometimes with ice.

For lunch I will have a salad or just vegetables with a piece of bread.

For dinner I will have baked chicken or fish with vegetables and salad.

Exercise

It is very important to exercise as well to benefit the body. As with anything this takes commitment coupled with accountability. I struggle to maintain an exercise regimen. But I realize the benefits that propels me into action. The benefits of exercise as we all know are strengthened muscles, it combats disease, and is a way to manage your weight. The biggest benefit I have yet to mention though is sweating that is an avenue to detoxify the body. I don't want to over exaggerate this. Sweat only carries a minute amount of toxins out of the body (scientist state it is less then one percent), but I still feel purified and cleansed after I have exercised, sweat, and drank water. It makes sense to exercise for this fact alone since we are exposed to so many toxins in our lives. My interest lies in detoxifying the body.

My interest also lies in increasing my physical endurance to be able complete a marathon. Right now I would be lucky to complete a 5k!

I also desire to become a certified personal trainer so I will possess the knowledge of knowing how to train for my own personal growth.

Respect the Earth

When I studied an environmental science class in college it changed my life. It taught me how to do more for our Earth. I was able to understand the importance of conservation, our food chain, ecosystems, renewable energy sources, and non-renewable energy sources. When we make choices in our lives each day we should make the best choice we can out of what is made available to us so that we will not harm the Earth.

In reality, we can't all go "green" in every aspect of our lives because we can't afford it. But I will share with you what I do. I know it may seem repetitious because it is probably things you have heard before, but I still think it is worth repeating.

I shop with a reusable shopping bag. I get mad at myself at times because I walk right out of the front door of my home and forget to take it with me. In those cases, I reuse the plastic bags for garbage bags. Even though I do reuse the plastic bag(s), I do not like using them because plastic takes up to 500 years to degrade in our environment.

I try to buy recycled products when I can afford it. As an example, recycled toilet paper. The toilet paper is made out of recycled paper, therefore, it preserves our forests.

If you look for recycled products you would be amazed at what you will find. Once I found recycled shoe laces!

I try to buy organic food when I can afford it also. Organic food is grown with no pesticides. Pesticides are harmful to our environment. There are risks to wildlife and it causes plant toxicity.

I changed all of my incandescent light bulbs to fluorescent light bulbs. This conserves energy, thus, producing less carbon emissions.

I try to unplug all of my electronics before I leave my home for the day. Even when something is plugged in and turned off it is still using energy.

I turn off my hot water tank after showering. It reduces the use and cost of energy, too.

I save food that is left over from dinner and eat all my leftovers. In other words, I do not waste food. This reduces my carbon footprint by not having to purchase food that uses valuable resources to get the product to me.

Once I made a huge pot of vegetable soup and my son and I ate vegetable soup and grilled cheese sandwiches for an entire week! He got so tired of the soup, but I do not waste.

A friend of mine thinks I am over the top with how obsessed I am with saving food. She tried to patronize my economizing when we had gone to a movie and I had popcorn left over by asking me if I was going to freeze my popcorn! I may be obsessive, but I do not waste!

I try to eat low on the food chain. If you eat more vegetables than meat, again, it takes less natural resources to get the product to you. You can find wonderful tasting vegetarian chicken nuggets, vegetarian corn dogs, vegetarian pizza, vegetarian sub sandwiches, and vegetarian soups that can substitute for meat consumption.

Recycle. I recycle batteries, plastic bottles, newspaper, cardboard, and aluminum cans. Recycling aluminum cans is great because it gives you a few extra dollars in your pocket! I like the benefits of this type of going "green"!

Reduce, Recycle, and Reuse

NOTES

Principle #3: Know what you like and do not like

You must know what you like and dislike to move forward toward any goal. We must develop ourselves to gain a deeper perspective of what we believe and want for ourselves. Sometimes we may get in the way of the things we want. If we assess our belief system along with our daily, weekly, short term, and long term commitments, we can understand what may be preventing us from obtaining what it is we are trying to achieve. If you want to sing you must begin by practicing; you must train your voice, and/or take voice lessons. If your not doing something every day toward your goal, you will not achieve them. As previously stated, achieving goals is the art of discipline. I remain disciplined by remaining accountable to myself. I do this by making a list of things I need or want to accomplish each day to move me closer in the direction of my goals. If I fall short, I reassign, not resign, what I did not accomplish to the agenda for the following day by committing myself to that particular priority. Even though I may be disappointed at my lack of progress, I always leave room for the adjustment of my goals. But I also always approach my list with the expectation of fulfillment.

On the following pages is a Personal Value Assessment questionnaire that may help you to reflect upon and develop a sense of who you. The point of taking this assessment is to possibly provide you with oversimplified answer sheet in finding your "niche" in life.

Permission has been granted for this questionnaire to be reproduced in this book for the purpose of it being a teaching tool.

PERSONAL VALUES ASSESSMENT:

What are your main values in life?

What is the most important value to you?

What difficult life experience had the greatest impact on you?

What past experience brought you the most joy?

What are your natural strengths?

22

What activity do you enjoy so much that you can lose all track of time?

If you could go and do anything in the world you wanted to, what would it be?

When did you last accomplish something you thought was very significant?

NOTES

Principle #4: Challenge yourself to keep a vision

By challenging yourself you remain a visionary. How do you challenge yourself? Remaining accountable to your goals through motivation. What is the difference in motivation and inspiration? Where the accountability lies. Inspiration lies with others; motivation lies with an individual.

As we have already defined, inspiration is an example, opportunity, and/or knowledge to achieve a goal (through others—and God). To repeat, by challenging yourself you remain a visionary. How do you challenge yourself? Remaining accountable to yourself.

Motivation is you taking action or moving toward your goal. You must act upon what you desire. To reiterate, I keep myself motivated by making a list of things I want to accomplish each day. I break down the goal into manageable segments and decide upon a desired completion date. When I decided to write this book, I knew I wanted to have it completed within a certain time frame. So each day I worked on it. You must break down what it is you want to accomplish into small steps.

It is also important to document your progress. It keeps you focused while maintaining the desire. If you see progress, reward yourself!

I love second hand stores. I buy jeans, and shirts second hand (this helps the environment, too). But what I also love are the books, knick knacks, and paintings. Once I paid two dollars for a replicate of the painting "Prima Ballerina" by Edgar Degas. I had it appraised and it was worth five hundred dollars!

As a way to reward myself, I set a five dollar spending limit to purchase something at a second hand store.

Keeping yourself motivated is really managing your life with passion. You can create passion by choosing to be happy, by knowing who you are, and what you want. But passion does not always make you feel happy. None of us feel happy one hundred percent of the time. The key is remaining consistent, you will then be rewarded by the fruits of your labor, in which one *is* feeling happy.

Once I set a goal and achieved it. Afterward I felt a void. I could not understand why I did not feel happier.

For one, I realized it was the process of achieving the goal that had given me pleasure.

Secondly, as already stated, what you achieve with motivation does not always make you feel happy.

Thirdly, I had not set a vision beyond what life would be like after I had achieved the goal. In other words, I had not prepared or informed myself with an accurate depiction or expectation of what life would be like after the temporal success of that particular goal.

To feel as you have purpose, you need to *create* purpose by setting goals for yourself daily, weekly, monthly, yearly, *and beyond what you will do after you have achieved your goal.* There is a fine line to this in what I am wanting to convey because I know it sounds as if I am advocating not being happy with who you are since you are constantly reaching for more. What I am trying to relate is just the opposite. So let me expand to include a broader definition of what success means.

Success means sustained happiness *with* success and *after* achievement.

Is goal setting why someone can be happy in the midst of adversity? Or be happy when they have not achieved their dream(s)? Or have continued happiness once they have achieved a dream? And are content even though they live in a mobile home and not a mansion? Yes, this person has adopted a winning attitude into their psyche.

Success is an overcoming spirit that sees and rewards yourself for the things you have accomplished, which gives you the ability to love and appreciate those things beyond measure without wanting or feeling as if you need more.

This attitude is what allows you to live in the moment and be content with the things you have . . . . but it also allows you to press forward when you want to reach for higher goals.

This ability is what allows you to appreciate the same in others.

Developing this ability ceases social and economic divide.

Success does not see age either. Success is available at anytime or at any age. You can be five or fifty and birth a vision to see it to its completion Therefore, we should shift our cultural mentality to value the importance of a person's worth through their *entire* life span. We should exhibit this shift of thinking by offering continuous opportunities for individuals regardless of age. This would help keep motivation, focus, and passion in lives, thus, reducing illnesses associated with having no purpose (e.g., depression).

I am forty three years old and am just now beginning to achieve dreams I once dreamed as a child.

If it had not of been for certain pageant systems increasing the age limit of women, I would had not qualified to compete in some at my age (being 43 years old I am placed in the senior division and my eighteen year old son gets a kick out of it!). Thank you to those who have!

Transitioning back to the feeling of unhappiness I felt after I had achieved one of my goals, I had to answer what was I lacking to have made me feel this way? My answer: A more mature perspective. Or perhaps I just needed reorientation to the person I already was and had gotten out of touch with.

NOTES

Principle #5: Pray for guidance when you feel lost

There have been many times in my life where hurt broke my focus and I felt lost. I did not want to move forward. Nor did I know how. Life seemed pointless. Moving forward, with maintaining a positive attitude intact to get me to the "other side" seemed far out of reach. I was so negative in my thoughts.

I have found when I have not known what to do I pray for guidance. Praying for guidance has never failed me. I do not automatically have an immediate understanding, instantaneous direction, or clarity in my life, but what I do have is an awareness I will eventually know what to do. Prayer helps me to believe in the impossible and to develop problem solving skills. I know you are asking if you are doing the work then why believe in a God? Again, it is for the inspiration or the example, knowledge, and/or opportunity that only God can provide.

Personally, I do believe our dependence upon God and who we think God is has been distorted. My belief about how God operates in our universe in relation to being in "control" is only by providing guidance. I do not think God is in control of actions, deeds, words and/or outcomes of an individual life. How I believe God is in control is by showing us how to apply the principles of a Godly life He has ordained. These principles I believe are to love ourselves, others, and the Earth. It is the *results* of applying these principles that are Godly outcomes that define God being in control.

Don't get me wrong. I do believe God is all knowing. But not in the sense of knowing the details of *every* person's life. I believe God is all knowing only in the sense of having all knowledge of how things operate in our universe (i.e., what happens in general when we violate or don't violate any universal laws). Again, these "things" that make God all knowing is by understanding the totality of the application of universal laws.

Don't get me wrong about this either. I may have misstated something. I do believe God can know the details of a person's life, but I think it is only when a person comes to God and asks for guidance. God can then show that person how to improve their life through inspiration, but as previously stated we must do the work. I believe we are held accountable for our lives or the action taken to improve it.

Why is there a God if God does not get involved? God *is* involved by the existing infinite knowledge given to us through life principles to help us to change, and grow. But there is more to be learned than the general principles we may understand at the moment because knowledge with God is never ending. So the potential for growth is never ending. We become more like God when we learn to make decisions as God would make decisions through the application of selfless principles towards ourselves, others, and the Earth.

NOTES

MY MOBILE HOME BEFORE THE RENOVATIONS

My Mobile Home After Renovations. What A Difference!

Principle #6: Persevere during unexpected happenings

It is hard to remain focused when unexpected events change your circumstances that moves you in an opposite direction away from your goal. How do you get back on track? By understanding the totality of what success is:

Success is also sustained effort in the midst of adversity.

What is it called when you *do* achieve a goal? Achievement. You have executed the task of success to completion.

What do you do if the grievances in life alter your life course? Success again is another word for hope, being positive, or motivated (refer back to principle #4), with each of these things multitasking with problem solving skills. Success is a life skill that enables us to overcome our challenges. So even if grievances changes your direction or desires, success enables us to remain focused and persevere toward the same or new desired goal.

Grievances do change us and although I do not think it is meant for us to suffer, I believe if we embrace it, we can broaden our perspective. I will tell you a story about my life.

At the age of seventeen, my parents divorced. I was actually three months shy from my eighteenth birthday.

The divorce reeked financial havoc on our family and my mother and I ended up homeless. We lived anywhere from our car to family or with friends. It was humbling and I began to harbor anger toward my mother for the way my life was (later in life when I began my search for healing I realized harboring anger is caused from unmet needs. I later forgave my mother; I do not blame my parents for the divorce).

My mother was lost after the divorce because all she had ever known was being a housewife until I attended junior high school (now called middle school). That is when she entered the workforce.

My mother was successful in the workforce. She worked in retail and it did not take her long to obtain management level. When she began a new job, it seemed it only took a matter of weeks before she was being offered a promotion. But even though she worked, it was just to help out. She never learned how to be the bread winner. My mother was born in 1936 and the role of a woman was much,

much different than what it is today. My father was the one who was head of the household. When my parents divorced, she was a displaced homemaker.

I went through a lot of emotional trauma having no stability that was created from the divorce. Although we were helped by individuals and had places to live temporarily, at times we were still treated less than human because of our circumstances. It created such a need in me of just wanting to be loved . . . . or what I think, it created a deeper need in me to *give* my love. As a result, I misjudged using my gifts and made many sexual mistakes. I condemned myself for the longest time for my misjudgments because, for me, being with more than one sexual partner during my lifetime was just too many. I only wanted to be with *one* person my entire life. Sexual purity had been taught to me by my mother . . . and again, I personally believed in it. In our home, sexual purity was defined as: Sharing your body with only one person your entire life. And to use sexual intercourse not as a means for physical pleasure, but as a means to show someone how much you loved them. Therefore, when I thought I was in love, I gave myself to the man I loved.

But Mother also taught us to save ourselves for marriage.

It is a little more complicated than just this simplified explanation, but for the purpose of this book, this is mostly why I condemned myself, too.

Being naïve at the age of 20 (not from believing in a false assumption from what sexual intercourse meant, but from falsely believing in honorable intentions from men), I became pregnant. And at the age of 25 I became pregnant again. My second pregnancy was the turning point in my life. I wanted to change my life. This slow process began by me taking responsibility for my life . . . by looking from within. You must first examine yourself internally before changes can be made externally. Why? *Thoughts*, words, and deeds are so powerful. They manifest themselves outwardly to create life for you from what it is you feel. I had to ask myself what it was I thinking, feeling, and doing to have created the life I had. When you are earnest in your quest, you can have self-discovery because a higher power in our universe wants us well.

What I discovered, I had more grief than what I had realized. My maternal grandmother had passed away a few months prior to my parents divorcing and I had not grieved over the loss of her because things had spun out of control so quickly when my parents divorced.

The grief from the loss of my grandmother was also intertwined with the loss of my family dynamic being broken, and from my sexual innocence being no longer intact. As I stated, remaining a virgin until I was married was something that was very, very important to me. Coming to terms with no longer being a virgin, especially compounded with being a single mother was very, very difficult for me. It had affected the love I had for myself. I did not like myself. I felt "used" and dirty.

As a child growing up I had been so happy. I loved my parents and they loved me. They supported me with the things I wanted to do. I had a wonderful childhood. My parents deserve a tribute.

The worst thing I had to deal with in my childhood was not feeling pretty and being *abnormally* shy. I was more than an introvert. I was a total geek. I wanted to be more extroverted and I wanted to be beautiful. That is why I began competing in pageants at the age of 16. The first pageant I entered was the Pensacola Easter Queen Pageant. My second pageant was the Miss Florida National Teenager Scholarship Pageant. As you probably guessed, I did horrible at both!

I did not compete again until the age of eighteen when I began competing in pageants full time. I did well in some and horrible in others. My confidence was always up and down. As I previously mentioned, I was abnormally shy so my nerves were unpredictable. Even to this day I continue to struggle with nervousness on stage to an abnormal extent.

After the birth of my first child I only competed in a few pageants.

After the birth of my second child I did not compete for eleven years, from 1992-2003.

From 2003 to the present, I have competed in six pageants.

Why have I continued to compete if I feel so uncomfortable on stage? There are two reasons. First, I wanted to face (and possibly conquer) my fears. Secondly, I wanted to be given a platform to promote the causes I believe in. What do I believe in? One cause I believe in is building the self-esteem of young girls so they will love themselves *from within*.

Have I succeed at these goals? One yes, the other No.

Facing my fears by competing on stage has allowed me to experience failure many times. It left me with many unsuccessful attempts—even as most recent as 2012. The outcomes were always the same: stage fright, lack of concentration from nerves, dry mouth, and an uneasy gait, that resulted in me not placing. What *has* been successful is what I learned about myself. It confirmed what I had already begun realizing as a teenager: My lack of skills for competing in pageants is innate. Allow me to explain the difference between lack of ability and limited ability so you will understand my gifts.

Limited ability can't grow because you don't have the natural (inherent) ability for it to be nurtured.

Lack of ability can grow if it is nurtured.

My skills are limited. Therefore, competing in pageants has only helped me grow as a person, not perfect public speaking skills, or develop skills to engage an audience (as I have seen it do for other girls). In other words, I blossomed on the inside, not the outside, which is precisely why others think I am still a novice with pageants—and are surprised I am not more poised, given my experience.

I am limited in my ability because I cannot overcome or conquer.

As a teenager my vision of what I wanted to accomplish through pageants was to gain poise, learn beauty tips, and for the competitiveness of winning the crown. But now that I am much, much older pageants have helped me to develop an enlarged vision—to include helping others.

My goal is to change the perception of beauty. That is why I founded the Miss U.S. Inner Beauty Pageant. This pageant judge contestants on inner beauty and not outward beauty because first, I want to judge what is coming out of the heart and not what is being displayed on stage. This is why I personally became interested in online or mail in pageants.

Secondly, it is an opportunity for girls and women who are just like me—introverted, but yet dares to dream—and tries to overcome. You don't have to have public speaking skills, confident stage presence or have to even promote the title to win. *This is an opportunity to win something to increase the positive manner in which you view yourself.* This is why I personally became interested in online or mail in pageants.

Thirdly, I understand physical beauty is fleeting. My perspective on beauty (and pageants) is this: Physical beauty can be enhanced with makeup but most generally a naked face is plain. I grant you there are exceptions but the average woman is just that . . . . average. Yes, makeup, as well as hair, can enhance beauty but it is an *illusion*. Even the most gifted girl doesn't look drop dead gorgeous until her hair and makeup are done. Let me demonstrate.

In one pageant I competed in I thought I had a great chance of winning the photogenic competition. I know I will sound conceded, but I was very proud of my picture.

Having a good photogenic picture to me is recognizing yourself in the picture to look as you do in person. In other words, I like natural beauty to shine through. Well, the girl who won looked *nothing* like her photograph in person. In the photograph she had a lot of makeup on and her hair was slicked back that made her unrecognizable in person. From that experience I learned what pageants should not be and what modeling should be. Being a model should not mean being beautiful. It should be glamorized to mean having a face that is chameleon like. In other words, a person needs to have a face that has the ability to be altered into many different looks . . . and not a face that is drop dead gorgeous.

Modeling should be defined as art.

Pageants should be a teaching tool for young girls to empower them to be comfortable with themselves BUT it has to begin with judging a contestant on natural beauty in all phases of competition. Natural beauty or being "beautiful" should be defined as looking YOUR best regardless of imperfections.

Pageants should also be a teaching tool within society to differentiate the meaning of what being a model is and what being beautiful isn't.

Pageants that are looking for glamorous or high fashion faces and photos should be called a *modeling pageant* and not a beauty pageant (I am aware these types of pageants are currently called Glitz pageants, but I still think we should make the distinction by it being called a modeling pageant. This distinction was not made in some pageants I have competed in, therefore, I did not know what they were looking for). When we begin setting standards for beauty that can only be attained through modeling, our perceptions of what beauty is is then distorted. In modeling, you are transforming yourself into something you are NOT.

No one can obtain the level of beauty that is shown in modeling without help.

If a young girl aspires to look like a model what they are really aspiring to become is a canvass for a makeup artist; someone to apply makeup to make a person appear different that what they look naturally.

I do want you to know I don't see anything wrong with looking your best (with hair and makeup). But we also must be careful to not become obsessed trying to look our best either.

What I am promoting is looking your best that will help you move forward to be the best you can be from the inside out.

Being obsessed is being selfish.

Looking your best is taking care of yourself.

I try to take care of myself with giving great care to my skin so I will age gracefully. I admit I use Botox between my eyebrows and under my eyes. I give myself facials, exfoliate, and moisturize daily. But I know I am not perfect nor is my life perfect as others try to suggest when they are representing "beauty" . . . . but I still love myself.

I have learned to love myself even though I have made bad decisions in my life, I am not rich, I lack public speaking skills and stage presence, I have a bald spot in my hair (my hair is also grey in some areas), I inherited dark circles under my eyes from my grandmother and mother, I wear my hair up the majority of the time and I only wear it down for special occasions or when competing in a pageant, I have a crazy natural part in the front of my hair that looks like a the letter V, I prefer to wear jeans, t-shirts and sweatshirts, and I am getting old that is beginning to show its signs on my face. Even though I don't fit the cookie cutter mold of a beauty queen and I have the flaws I listed above, I still have been able to achieve my dreams. Why? Being myself. It is because of my flaws others have been able to see the true beauty I possess that has defined who I am and has allowed me to achieve.

Be yourself, believe in yourself, and improve yourself, but don't change yourself! Perfection is not beauty without flaws; it is being happy and being YOU!

I believe the purpose of pageants have long been misunderstood and we have gotten away from the original intent. I believe the conception of pageants was a way to develop the whole man by judging a contestant on the three components that make up a person—mind (intelligence displayed in interview), body (physical fitness displayed through evening gown and/or swimsuit), and soul (care given to others by being involved in the community/volunteering). This is what true beauty was supposed to mean . . . and what we have (again) gravitated away from.

Just know you do not have to be beautiful (or an eloquent speaker) to create change for others (or to even win a pageant). Alternatively (for me) I found I can put my words in print to create change for others to avoid public speaking because of my limited skills. Writing has been my best gift to accomplish what I want in life, again, given my limited abilities. This is why I personally became interested in online or mail in pageants.

Let's get back on track . . . When I began my search for self-discovery after the birth of my second child, the first thing I realized was *you attract what and who you are.*

When I was in the two different relationships with my sons fathers, I was broken and hurting so I attracted the same type of men. Of course my life was a mess after they exited my life because we both only had part of ourselves to give. The other parts were mired in dysfunction from the things we *both* had not dealt with and were still carrying around.

Secondly, I realized *if I wanted my life to change I needed to take responsibility for my actions and stop blaming and playing the victim.* I don't want to minimize the affect others had on my life (or yours) from their actions. But there comes a point when you realize what actions others have taken or decisions others have made do not have to control your life. It may have affected your life, but it doesn't have to destroy, or stagnant your life.

To change your life make decisions with self-control, self-discipline, and self-respect for yourself and others.

When I was pregnant with my first child, a close personal friend of the family, who was a teacher, helped my mother and me get into low income housing. I lived in low income housing until after the birth of my second child. I wanted desperately something more for my life. So each week I put aside money, little by little, out of my paychecks for a down payment on a mobile home. I think when I had saved $500, I began my search. With the help of a loan officer that believed in me, I was approved a loan for a 3 bedroom, 1 bathroom mobile home. It was one of the happiest days of my life. I no longer had to live under the stigma of living in government housing . . . but now I was living under the stigma of living in a mobile home. There were other reasons involved as to why I bought a doublewide mobile home a few years later after having purchased the singlewide 3 bedroom, 1 bathroom mobile home, but part of the reason I wanted a doublewide instead of a singlewide mobile home was so that it would appear as if I had a house and not a mobile home. Doublewides look more like houses. I felt bad about myself that I was living in a single wide mobile home. I did not feel "good enough".

A few years later, due to financial circumstances, I had to down size to a single wide once more. This mobile home was the pits. It was a handy man special. There were roaches everywhere and a huge rat living in it. I had to gut it and remodel its entirety. I did contract some of the work that needed to be done, but I also did some of the work myself. Each day I seen progress, I became more and more excited. I fell in love with this ugly mobile home, that was now turning into something beautiful. Why was it different for me this time? *I was beginning to love myself (again).* Since I had put my heart and soul into the project of it being remodeled, it was a reflection of who I was. I value, and respect my home, because I value and respect who I am. I still live in this mobile home today and have for the past twelve years. Sure it is getting old. It is not perfect. The paint inside is beginning to slightly crack in places, I never finished replacing the tile on the bathroom floor, and the outside needs a little more work, but nothing is without flaws.

This mobile home became representative of what I had to overcome in my life.

I recently had a friend from work come over to help repair something at my home and he told someone at work it wasn't that nice. It stung. It hurt because I felt he was blind for one (I personally think it is nice), but more importantly I felt he wasn't recognizing my success. Remember, success is sustained effort in the midst of adversity. My adversity had been being homeless, being a single mother, with no education at the time, and working a full and part time low paying job to make ends meet . . . but I overcame it all.

Success isn't a Mercedes or a mansion nor is the measure of success determined by where someone lives or what someone drives. Success is determined by an overcoming spirit.

For me, I am proud of my accomplishments. My sustained effort afforded me with a mobile home that I presently live in. Having to rebuild this home from the inside out was mimicking the portrait of my life because I was in transition of rebuilding my soul; rebuilding my life from the inside out.

I believe simplicity is the key to strip a person of pretense. Therefore, be proud of who you are and where you come from. Inner beauty is success. What you do with it will be your accomplishments.

As you have already noted, I am not rich nor were my parents. My mother as I have already written was in retail sales and also owned a part time cleaning business. My father was in the military (he was in the reserves the last ten years of his career) and worked as one of the supervisors in shipping and receiving at our port.

Being a descendent from them was more valuable than being born with a silver spoon in my mouth because it is partly due to them why I am the person I am (the other part, I owe myself the credit). The values of sexual purity, hard work, discipline, loving someone from what they have to offer from within, are all examples of things that were taught to me.

One reason my life had turned out the way it had is because my thinking had been manipulated because *the people I involved in my life weren't the things I had become or believed in: sexual purity, hard work, discipline, and loving someone from what they have to offer from within.*

The other reasons were of my own doing, therefore, I was confused and no longer knew who I was. As a result, I wasn't able to understand my worth. I began to understand my worth when I began to look within. As I already knew and rediscovered, *your value comes from within.* I overcame my circumstances because I realized I didn't have to stay where I was. Below are the formulas that recap what I have stated thus far:

Confidence + Ability = Opportunity for Accomplishments

Value (the qualities that you have from within) + Respect (the love you have for yourself, others and the Earth)= Beautiful

Success (sustained effort in the midst of adversity) + Motivation (taking action toward a goal) = Accomplishments

One more notation . . . when you pray for guidance (Principle #5) during unexpected happenings, unexpected happiness follows. In 2008 a homeless cat showed up at my doorstep. I fell in love with her and decided to keep her. I named her Kitty (very original I know). She was pregnant and had a litter of kittens. I don't understand what happened to her but she went missing. As a result, her kittens were abandoned so my son and me took care of them; we bottle fed them and once they were old enough we gave them all away but one. The one we kept, I called him Little Guy because he was the runt of the litter. Although he later came up missing, too, (I cried for days when I could not find him) he became such a big part of our family the time he was with us. He brought so much love to us. I felt like he had been a gift from God (just like Kitty had been) because the universe gave him to me. That is how you know when something is from a higher universal presence . . . when you are not looking and a gift is bestowed upon you.

I believe God gave him to me because I was going through a very difficult time in my life and I had been praying for God to help me. I had only had Little Guy in my life for approximately five weeks when my mother had to be admitted into the hospital for a simple procedure, but took a turn for the worse and ended up in ICU on life support with pneumonia and a fractured hip. I did not go to work for five days because I sat at her bedside holding her hand trying to help her pull through. I cried everyday and it to put it lightly, it took its toll on me.

I had just began a temporary part time job, too, for extra money and my coworkers were very difficult people to work with that exacerbated my stress.

I was terrified my mother was going to die. During the hours I could not be with her, I would go home and try to rest but I would end up sobbing for hours . . . and Little Guy was there to hold as I let my tears fall. At times he licked my tears away . . . just what I needed. It was if as he was there for me . . . as if God was there for me. My mother pulled through.

Never underestimate the power of the universe.

NOTES

Principle #7: Live your life with integrity

When we think of what integrity means, we tend to think of it as living a life not deluded by imperfection. We judge a person's character by their integrity. When they do make a mistake, we judge them harshly because of what we feel they have (mis)represented to us about their life.

Integrity does mean living your life with your best efforts. But what it does not mean is living your life without faltering. To simplify it, it means living your life purposefully by taking responsibility for *both* the good and bad that you do.

It may seem with this particular type of thinking it gives a person latitude to do what he or she wants because it enables the absence of real accountability since all a person has to do is "take responsibility". Integrity is just the opposite.

Accountability can be earnest when a person's intentions behind an action are understood.

If a wrong decision has been made based upon good intentions and the outcome was negative and you take responsibility for it, that shows integrity.

Lack of integrity or having lack of this characteristic is exhibited when you make a decision with bad intentions and it has a negative effect and you may or may not take responsibility.

Or if the result has been from a wrong decision based upon good intentions with *no* responsibility, this exemplifies a lack of integrity, too.

Again, to restate, integrity is a person's intentions coupled with responsibility. This could also be defined as having a conscience.

Integrity is shown when a person takes responsibility for their decisions and actions.

Integrity is also shown when good intentions are used *first* to make a decision. Good intentions are used from the *very* beginning.

Can anyone obtain integrity? Is it a characteristic, skill, or, attribute? And what is the difference between responsibility and accountability?

I do think the inclination towards integrity can be genetic. But I also believe you can orient yourself toward developing the skills of having integrity by asking yourself each time before you make any decision if it will hurt you, others, or the world around us.

The difference between accountability and responsibility is this:

Accountability is understanding what intentions were used to make a decision (either negative or positive).

Responsibility is trying to reduce the effect of any negative outcome as a result of your negative or positive intentional decision making. As an example, you could do this by an apology, changing your decision, restitution, or recompense.

If our intentions were positive from the onset, and if the outcome is negative, some things can be reversed. It is when we use our intentions negatively we destroy things that the effects remain irreversible.

Accountability (the intentions that are used to make a decision; it can be negative or positive) +

Responsibility (reducing the effect of any negative or positive intentional decisions by an apology, changing your decision, restitution, or recompense)

= Integrity (living your life purposefully by taking responsibility for both the good and bad that you do)

NOTES

Principle #8: Do not manipulate life to the benefit of your outcome

When you are not honest in your life or you cheat to win, to me that is the definition of blasphemy of God.

A person that is manipulating the circumstances in their life in their favor without letting life play out on its own alters the course of their life and that of others.

A person that cheats sets themselves up for reaping what they have sown because they have violated universal laws. These are laws I believe the Earth was intended to operate from and when we take no care towards them upon making a decision, or operate within the realm of violating them, we suffer the consequences of our *own* actions (and not the actions of a God that wants to punish us). Why? We did not adhere to (spiritual) principles.

God does not condemn or punish us. God only judges us.

Condemnation means to make you feel less than you are worth.

Judgment is to show you what you ARE worth.

What are spiritual principles? Making a decision with positive intentions by asking if it will hurt yourself, others, or the world around us.

How do we know this is "the" universal law? Who said so? How did someone realize this was a universal law? The way history has played out, the enlightenment of spiritual leaders, and through personal experiences. We have learned what has worked and what has not worked from the mistakes of others and ourselves. For me, it gives me peace to know things aren't left to chance, meaning, there is an order to our universe and when I do my part, the universe will do its part.

Understanding life principles helps us to navigate through life, to understand who God really is, and the effect of our active responsibility of our lives within the universe.

NOTES

Principle # 9: Give to your community

I remember at the age of sixteen I was driving home with my father and we passed a homeless man holding a cardboard sign that read, "Homeless. Will work for food." It was inclement weather and I felt so sorry for him. When we got home, I asked my father if I could give him one of our umbrellas. My father agreed to it but he told me to keep in my forethought that some homeless people were dishonest. He told me these particular type people were individuals that did not want to work and used the appearance of being homeless to panhandle money. I was saddened that someone would deceive others that way. I still took the umbrella to the homeless man, who expressed much gratitude, but wondered if I had really done a "good deed".

It's hard to know the intentions of others that appear as if they are in need. What my father made me aware of has not deterred me from helping others. If others had been jaded with such thinking when I was homeless, my mother and me would have not been helped.

But my father wasn't jaded, he was just realistic. I have learned there *are* dishonest people but when your intentions aren't it still spreads goodwill.

Being involved with helping others is important because it is reflective of what discipleship is. We are to help others to enable them to turn around to help others, too. We are mimicking the good deeds of Christ. This is why helping within our communities is so important. It is reaping what you sew. I may sound as if I have my head in the clouds, but I believe if we each did something toward solving the problems in our world we could achieve a Utopia.

In 2008, my youngest son and I helped feed the homeless in our community. From week to week, which was inclusive of a group of selfless people, we alternated who bought and/or prepared the food. At the end of the year, clocking over one hundred volunteer hours, we were each rewarded with the Bronze Presidential Volunteer Service award. I mention that only because it is proof no good deed goes unnoticed.

This year I have decided to focus my energies elsewhere. I have founded L.O.V.E. for children. This is a project that will provide monies, through the profit sales of specialty merchandise, to help rebuild schools within the United States. The acronym stands for liberty, opportunity, value, and equality (for children). I want to provide children the chance for a quality education to secure a better future. It all begins with a High School Diploma.

I want to stress being involved in your community can be as simple as supporting your favorite charity with as little as a one dollar donation. I am also a founding member of the Martin Luther King, Jr. Memorial Project in Washington, D.C. and a member of the Poverty Law Center in Montgomery, Alabama. Their intent is achieving equality; to lessen hatred and discrimination (to learn more go to www.mlkmemorial.org and www. splcenter.org).

In closing this chapter, keep in mind *if everyone did something toward solving the problems in our world we could change it.* We could extract and eradicate certain social problems. All we need is a vision, to get involved, and our visions could then become a reality.

NOTES

Principle #10: Just do it!

I know it is easy for others to tell you just to do it when your life is in shambles. You may be a single mother, homeless, or broke just as I was. I had to do whatever it took to help myself get back on my feet. I had to work two jobs, sometime three jobs, to even get close to kind of life I wanted. I am a dreamer and along the way there have been others to question my mental stability because they questioned if I was living in reality. I wasn't because I refused to accept the reality of the way my life was. *I lived as though my dreams were.* In other words, *I had hope.*

Goal setting is a way to create a deeper level of happiness or to conquer unhappiness.

Live the vision you have for life as though it were!

It does take hard work, innovation, and ingenuity to change circumstances. But it also takes help. If it had not been for the help of my mother I would not have been able to accomplish the things I have. She babysat for me, cooked meals, and did laundry.

It is so important to have support. If you don't have any family members to help you, I encourage you to find resources within your community that will help you. If you need help, you may e-mail or write to me and I will try to assist you in your search.

What I am trying to awake in you through Principle #10 is the encouragement needed to take that first step towards the beginning of the kind of life you envision for yourself. You can do it if you change your way of thinking.

Remember, success is not achievements, but an overcoming spirit. Achievements are the results of success.

If you have a winning attitude, you will develop the problem solving skills needed to "think" your way through your challenges or strategize a plan to overcome your negative circumstances.

Others may disagree I am successful because my achievements include living in a mobile home, and I have continued to work more than one job even though I am now educated (I own my own business and am a licensed security officer at a private gated community).

I think it is a misfortune to them (not an injustice to me) to have this particular perception because they don't realize what being happy is . . . . recognizing and celebrating what it took to get me from where I was to where I am now.

I am not suggesting to you all of my problems have disappeared; that I don't ever worry about a bill or run short of money or that life is any easier being a single mother. In fact, it has gotten harder. For the past three years I have been managing my life with devastating news. My mother is living with Alzheimer's Disease. Each day I see how much the disease deteriorates her mind. It is so hard because I am loosing my mother. I am faced with her mortality . . . as well as mine. And honestly, it is tough. I have my days of complete sadness.

Her sickness also complicates my life to a certain degree because I no longer have her emotional or physical support. And I have the added responsibility of taking care of things for her that she can no longer take care of herself . . . but I am not complaining because the point I am trying to make for you is living your life with success does not make your life devoid of any more difficulties or devoid of ever feeling sadness again. What I am expressing to you is that you can manage disappointments or the challenges life brings to you through success . . . it sustains me through both the good and hard times . . . and I desire that for your life, too!

NOTES

Glossary of Terms

Accomplishments—the end result of success

Accountability—understanding what intentions were used to make a decision

Beauty Pageant—a competition for both genders that allows each gender to express the level of development they have for the whole man of mind, body, and soul through interview, evening gown and/or swimsuit, and community service; individuals should not be judged on physical beauty

Blasphemy—manipulating circumstances in life for the benefit of your outcome

Challenge—remaining accountable to goals through motivation

Condemnation—to make you feel less than what you are worth

<u>Inspiration</u>—the need for others to help us to grow into the person we want to become; a need for God

<u>Integrity</u>—living your life purposefully by taking responsibility for both the good and bad that you do

<u>Intellect</u>—the ability to understand one another; the depth of compassion one has for humanity

<u>Intelligence</u>—the capacity or how capable one is in using their intellect; the ability to apply thought and reason

<u>Judgment</u>—to show you what you ARE worth

<u>Model/Modeling</u>—having a face that is chameleon like; it does not mean being beautiful

<u>Motivation</u>—taking action or moving toward your goal; it is managing your life with passion

<u>Original Dream</u>—a vision of something you want to accomplish that has never been thought of

<u>Perfection</u>—happiness; it does not mean without flaws

<u>Relationship of Inspiration</u>—connecting to a universal presence through someone or directly connecting to a universal presence that enables one to achieve their goals

<u>Respect</u>—the love you have for yourself, others, and the Earth

<u>Shared Dream</u>—having the same goal as another individual

<u>Success</u>—sustained effort is the midst of adversity; it also means sustained happiness with success and after achievement

<u>Universal Laws</u>—proven principles of life that allows us to live in concert with the universe and if violated disrupts the ebb and flow in our life and others, e.g. respecting yourself, others, and the world around us

<u>Value</u>—the qualities you have from within

Formulas

Original dreams are:

Knowledge + Enlightenment = Discovery

Confidence + Ability = Opportunity for Achievements

Value (the qualities that you have from within) + Respect (the love you have for yourself, others, and the Earth = Beautiful

Success (sustained effort in the midst of adversity) + Motivation (taking action toward a goal) = Accomplishments

Accountability (the intentions that are used to make a decision; it can be negative or positive) +

Responsibility (reducing the effect of any negative or positive intentional decisions by an apology, changing your decision, restitution, or recompense) = Integrity (living your life purposefully by taking responsibility for both the good and bad that you do)

Pageant and Modeling Resume

2012 Ms. Florida US of America, Jacksonville, Florida; did not place

2009 America's Miss Elegant America's U.S. Pageant, Vicksburg, Mississippi; last place (4th runner-up)

2009 Level 1 certification pageant judge

2008 Ms. Florida North America (competed in nationals in Nashua, New Hampshire); won Supermodels with Style Award and was featured on page 83 in the April/May 2009 issue of Supermodels Unlimited Magazine

2005 Miss American Rose, online/mail in pageant; won local and state title, finished as a finalist nationally

2005 Miss Florida National Southern USA Pageant, Panama City, Florida; won state title

2003 Miss Northwest Florida Intercontinental Pageant, Panama City, Florida; did not place

1994 Judged Sunburst USA Pageant, Panama City, Florida

1992 Judged the Little Miss Chili Pepper Pageant, Panama City, Florida

1992 Valentine's Sweetheart Pageant, Panama City, Florida; won the title

1992 Miss Gulf Coast, Crestview, Florida; 1st runner-up

1992 Florida Patriot USA Pageant, Panama City, Florida; won state title

1992 Miss Panama City and Miss Florida Classical USA Pageant, Panama City, Florida; won local and state title (competed in national pageant in Biloxi, Mississippi; placed last)

1992 Miss Panama City Cover Miss USA, Panama City, Florida; second runner up

Kimberly L. Bonnell

1992 Livin' Doll Florida State Pageant, Panama City Beach, Florida ; won state title

1992 Supreme Glamour Miss of America, Panama City Beach, Florida, placed last

1991 Swimsuit model for an art class at Gulf Coast Community College, Panama City, Florida

1991 Miss Florida All American Girl Pageant, Ft. Walton Beach, Florida; won state title (competed in national pageant in White Plains, New York; placed last)

1991 Panama City Spring Angels Pageant, Panama City, Florida; third runner up

1991 Panama City Southern Miss Pageant, Panama City, Florida; second runner up

1991 Miss Gulf Coast Pageant, Pensacola, Florida; fourth runner up

1991 Miss Gold Pageant, Panama City, Florida; semi-finalist

1990 Riviera of the South August Beauty Queen Brochure Model, Panama City Beach, Florida

1990 Glamour Girl Model Search, Panama City, Florida; semi-finalist

1990 Miss Hemisphere Pageant, Panama City, Florida; last place

1989 Pensacola Cover Miss USA Pageant, Pensacola, Florida; first runner up

1989 Classy Lady Beauty Contest, Panama City Beach, Florida; won the title

1989 Miss Northwest Florida (Miss America Preliminary Pageant), Chipley, Florida; did not place

1988 Miss Panama City Cover Miss USA Pageant, Panama City, Florida; third runner up

1988 Seafood Indian Summer Princess Pageant (Miss USA Preliminary Pageant), Panama City, Florida; won Miss Photogenic

1988 Miss Northwest Florida (Miss America Preliminary Pageant), Chipley, Florida; won Miss Congeniality

1988 Classy Lady Beauty Contest, Panama City Beach, Florida; third runner up

1987 Miss Northwest Florida (Miss America Preliminary Pageant), Chipley, Florida; did not place

1987 Fashion show model for the "Winning Image" clothing store, Panama City, Florida

1985 Miss Florida National Teenager Pageant, Orlando, Florida; did not place

1985 Pensacola Easter Queen Pageant, Pensacola, Florida; did not place

Contact Information

Miss U.S. Inner Beauty Pageant

Kimberly L. Bonnell, Founder and Executive Director

PO Box 30012

Panama City, Florida 32405

Email: msusinnerbeautypageant@gmail.com

To learn more about L.O.V.E. for Children visit my website at www.missusinnerbeautypageant.com

Or you may write to:

L.O.V.E. for Children

PO Box 30012

Panama City, Florida 32401

About the Author

Kimberly L. Bonnell is the founder and executive director of the Miss US Inner Beauty Pageant.

Kimberly is certified Professional Life Coach, a Board Certified Biblical Counselor and is a member of the American Association of Christian Counselors.

Other titles available by this author

Periodicals Through Time:
A Collection of Youthful Writings,
www.authorhouse.com